Be Your Own Cat

by
Prof. Oddfellow

EX LIBRIS

How to
Be Your Own Cat

Saint Augustine

For Erwin Rudolf Josef Alexander Schrödinger.

Table of Contents

Every man is an animal.
Every head of a man is
the head of an animal.
—Augustus De Morgan

The animal in man, elevated,
is a thing unimaginable in its great
powers of service and of strength.
It will make you tremble when
you recognize the power that
has awakened within you.
The animal in yourself will
then be a king among the
animals of the world.
—Mabel Collins

Foreword:
There's a Cat at the
Center of the Universe

There's a cat at the center of the universe.

Obviously.

Schrödinger's cat. And according to this cat, you're in a box. Of course. The entire universe is a box of darkness and stars and some other stuff. You may be there or not there, alive or dead. You may love this cat or not. The cat is sorry not sorry.

Because the cat's mind is a ball of yarn. Except that yarn is made of equal parts mouse and sunlight, excitation and indolence, quantum enthusiasm and prey, silver bells, black matter, catnip and irony.

And you? You are a nanoflea, a human neutrino somewhere on the distant spiral paw of that cosmic yarn which is the mind of a cat. Unless you're not.

No matter. You exist by the grace of your cat. And by the silken magnanimity which your cat does not possess. But let's imagine that somewhere inside the obvious and galootish void of your loutish being you have an inner cat. Oh, if such a doltish fleshbag of a human could contain something so subtle and soft, something so evanescent, lithe and glimmering.

But imagine that your inner cat, supple and artful inside you, is both asleep and awake in a box the exact size of itself. Of course, to your cat, any universe is the exact size of your cat.

Obviously.

And this cat, watching and preening inside you,

wants its sheen and mindful not-mindfulness to be on the outside. A cat is always a Möbius strip, a bend of light, an ampersand of gravity. A cat is always a parable and a paradox.

But what is the difference between you and a cat? If you have to ask, you're not a cat.

And so this book—agile and quick, mysterious, surprising and sly as any cat—is not for you. It is for the cat that you are, the cat that you can be.

Of course you want to be your own cat. To be plain as even a blunderous sapiens could grasp: If you were your cat, you'd know that you'd always wanted to be your cat.

But each of the cat's nine lives is lived in nine dimensions and so this book is an introduction to feline physics, a mouser grimoire, a grimalkin guide, a siamese travelogue, a numinous catalogue of the non-Cartesian, a Manx how-to, a tabby joke book of recipes and kitten lore for the aspiring puss or tom, domestic ocelot, jaguar or lynx.

Yes, perhaps by now it is clear *why* you want to be your own cat. In this book, the erudite Professor Oddfellow, already always part shimmering and inscrutable cat, explains *how*. The only question, now, is *when*?

When you become your own cat, you will learn that *when* bends as spacetime bends to the immensity of planets, to the will of your own cat. Perhaps even now, you have already begun the journey to being your own cat. Even now your nimble tongue licks a paw as you begin to turn the first page...

—Gary Barwin
Hamilton, Ontario

The Name
Unanswered To

Choose a pet name to which you will never respond. Have your name be full of meaning so that its syllables carry something of your character and the ideal to which you wish to live up. Consider a name of antique regality, or of sprightly elegance, or of wild heroism, or of heavy dignity, or of aristocratic *sang-froid*. You may even adopt an entire string of ancient names of significance. When you hear this name called, allow the vibrations to bounce off your ears like a seagull's cry bounces off the face of a cliff. Be as unmoved by the sound of your name as the cliff is unaffected by the seagull.

Awareness of Four Corners, Four Directions

As you are aware of the cardinal's song and the pull it exerts upon your musculature, sit with closed eyes in a circle at the center of the room and feel the pull of the cardinal directions. To discover the direction East, be still and wait to sense the fire of the rising sun. To confirm the direction of East, be still and wait to sense the approach of twilight and its blanket of darkness in the West. By courtesy of these two directions, you will be oriented to North and South. For the sake of vigilance,

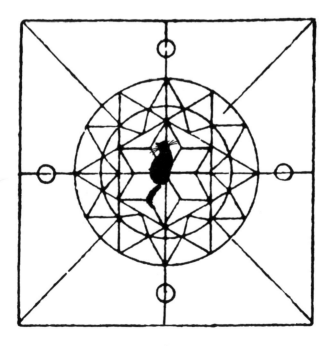

be also aware of the four corners of the room. Luxuriate in this awareness to your heart's content.

Be not discouraged if your progress is slow. Be not cast down if you slip back a step after having gained it. You will gain two at the next step. Let these be your affirmations:

- I am the center; around me revolves my world.
- I am the center of influence and power.
- I am the center of thought and consciousness.
- I am independent of my body; asleep I become a shadow.
- I am master of my mind, not its pet.
- I am invincible and cannot be injured.
- I am ninefold immortal and cannot be destroyed.

How to Use Mental Pictures to Create Felinity

What we mentally picture, we create. Imagination is the matrix of reality. Everyone wants to realize desires, but hardly anyone tries methodically to realize them in the imagination. Imagination wedded to concentration is the mother of reality. Here are important rules for the process:

1. Never concentrate on becoming your own cat immediately after dining upon pâté or drinking milk. The digestive functions for about an hour after each meal require all of one's surplus energy.

2. Fifteen or twenty minutes is long enough for each visualization session, two or three times a day. However, it is well to practice for a few minutes every hour if opportunities present themselves. The oftener you do this in your leisure moments, the quicker and more firmly will your ideal be absorbed and be made a part of your self. By this act you are appropriating the feline treasures that belong to you and bringing them into outward expression.

3. We grow to our ideals by first conceiving them. As images they may be somewhat shadowy and indistinct at first. Gradually, as we look at these mental pictures over and over again, we get them into perfect shape and form, until they reflect the ideal of what we would be and what we wish to be.

4. Perform your concentrations unseen as much as you can.

5. Much of the value of imagination depends on its vividness, as well as on its purity. The first step toward training the imagination is to observe the realities of life, to recall them immediately and then at intervals afterwards, and to establish them in memory. Out of these impressions of realities you can make up your imagination, altering the realities or the memories of them to form new pictures.

6. In all efforts to become your own cat through concentration, the mind should be in a well-poised, serene attitude. To accomplish this, breathe calmly, quietly, and leisurely. Leisureliness has nothing to do with laziness. Take long, deep, unhurried, rhythmical, yet easy and lithe breaths. To the popular mind, leisureliness does not suggest concentration. Even so, it means the highest concentration which does not lose sight of "first" things. Indeed, without leisureliness,

there cannot be ideal concentration, for concentration leads to control and economy of energy.

7. The more faith you have in the methods you employ, the greater your results, because faith invariably awakens higher and more powerful forces.

8. Positive statements may be combined with the process of concentration. For example, you may affirm, "I am constantly growing in my capacity to pounce."

9. Never begin concentration until you have refined yourself through bathing. Cleanliness is inseparable from felinity.

10. Never be overly anxious about results, because you know that results must inevitably follow. Don't consider that becoming your own cat will occur in an indefinite future but rather that your desired outcome is just awaiting your grasp. Draw yourself toward the image, recognizing that it is a reflection of your true self. By doing so you are binding your consciousness to your ideal felinity.

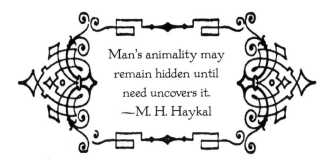

Man's animality may
remain hidden until
need uncovers it.
—M. H. Haykal

Qualities to Contemplate and to Cultivate

1. A cat relishes petting and fondling very highly but is soon satisfied. "Too much of a good thing" is studiously avoided.

2. A cat's quarrelsomeness is connected to great love of neatness, for the simple reason that a cat is "put out" when things are in disorder.

3. A cat is remarkably fond of play. A playful cat is honest, while a demure one is treacherous. Soft and quiet manners must be distinguished from gentleness.

4. A cat is sly. It is a cat's nature to take by surprise—a cat lives by it and therefore surprises others in everything, from entrances to absences.

Teaching the Floor to Talk

The floor has much to tell, once it has been taught to talk. It is said that teaching best occurs through shared experiences and that one's teaching is improved by listening to oneself and one's pupil. That's why lying upon the floor with open ears is crucial. When approaching something profoundly quiet, communication occurs when nonverbal behavior is given communicative intent by the listener. When you stretch out across the floor, you facilitate and guide the teaching and learning experience by initiating tactile communication.

Once you have heard what the floor has to say, allow more voices to converse—a table, a countertop, a chair, a step, and so on. It will be interesting to compare the different communication styles of brick, wood, tile, iron, slate, and concrete.

Lifting Oneself Toward the Summit of One's Dream

"I raise myself to this stand-point, and am a new creature. My whole relation to the existing world is changed. The ties by which my mind was heretofore bound to this world, and by whose secret attraction it followed all the movements of this world, are forever divided, and I stand free; myself, my own world, peaceful and unmoved. No longer with the heart, with the eye alone, I seize the objects about me, and, through the eye alone, am connected with them" (Johann Gottlieb Fichte, *The Destination of Man*, 1846).

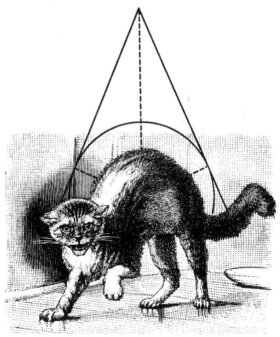

To Listen Without Seeming to Attend

Without seeming to pay attention, become familiar with the separate sounds in your environment. (Even if you are hard-of-hearing, attune to subtle vibrations and intuit the directions of their sources.) In this way you will form a clear conception not only of the various sounds themselves but also of their relation to one another and what they signify. Day after day, endeavor to distinguish the sources of each sound. Meditate upon the exact tone sounded by a bell, a breaking twig, a cuckoo bird. It is a severe mental exercise, but it yields the best results. Ear-training is thus a process of mind-training. Keeping a blank face during this training is simply part of being in full composure of oneself. Amidst uncertainties, one learns to listen without reacting.

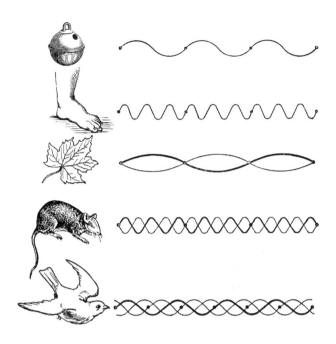

As Robert Schumann said, "We should learn to refine the inner ear," but refining the inner ear means training the mind to interpret aright the sound impulses that come to the brain through the outer ear. It means further to cultivate the mind's power to form clear and accurate conceptions of the tones which the outer ear reports, to judge correctly concerning them, and to develop the power of thought. Thus, ear-training is of the very first importance in becoming one's own cat.

The Invitation of
a Fireplace

A fireplace invites you to curl up in front of it. The pops, crackles, and hisses of burning wood embellish a mystery story about a mystery. Someone once said that the best story to tell is one that devours itself, and that is also true of the best story to hear. To prevent the story from devouring you, curl up close enough to feel the warmth of the fire but just far enough away not to become scorched. The best way to honor the fireplace's invitation is to stay for the entire story. If you fall asleep, that is perfectly within etiquette.

Why the Eye of the Mouse is a Gleaming Jewel

There are slow and fast areas in everything. A blank wall is of course a slow area. The surface of a pond, with poking turtle heads and fish mouths and ripples, is a fast area. The soft body of a mouse, like a gray cloud, is a slow area, while the ears, nose, hands, tail, and eyes are fast areas. The key to the entire mouse is the eye and where the eye is placed. It lies on each side of the head, balanced between the fast ears and fast nose. It's difficult to imagine the eye being anywhere else on the mouse's body. Close to the tail? Ridiculous. At the center of the back? Absurd. On the belly? Ludicrous. The eye is perfectly placed to display a jewel in the middle of the head. The eye is the focal point of the mouse. It is the mouse's eye that one must track. Find the jewel in other species of animal. Is it always the eye?

To Breathe, Perchance to Smell

Go to a place which is well hidden, where people or other animals will not come to disturb you. It is here, lying on the floor or sitting on a comfortable cushion, that you can best practice indrawing nature's vitality as a refined brain-food.

The mouth is closed during both inspiration and expiration, the nose being used for both the entrance and the exit of the air and the various aromas carried by it.

1. Inhale through the nostrils in a slow, steady draw, detecting all the scents you can.

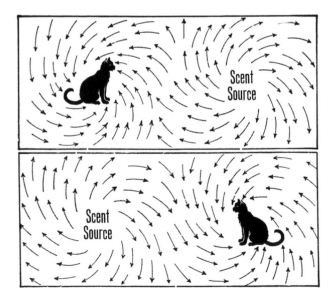

2. Hold this full breath for about four beats, allowing the aromas to linger in your nostrils.

3. Exhale slowly as you contemplate the nature of the smells.

4. Keep the lungs empty for a moment before continuing the exercise. With each separate inhalation, you will find yourself better able to identify individual scents.

To practice breathing-smelling while walking, sniff for two or three steps and then exhale for the next two steps. There is no hard and fast rule as to the number of sniffs. Adapt the system to your own liking.

After this exercise of conscious sniffing and mentally identifying aromas, investigate the aromas' origins. That will bring completion to the proper practice. Keep in mind that the nearest scent source may be behind you.

The Feline Way
of Harmony

Look for the highest accessible spot within your range of vision. That is where you will wish to sit, as a commanding view is a place of power. Upon reaching this spot, simply be attentive. This announces to the woods, meadow, mountains, river, or whatever the particular environment, that you are listening. You will hear sounds but also silence, which is not precisely the opposite of sound. Depending upon the weather, you will hear both the raining and the rained-upon, both the blowing and the blown-upon. You will hear insects at work and foliage growing. If you are indoors, you will hear the outside world interacting with the walls and roof. But none of these sounds is an end in itself. Listen for them, to be sure, but as parts of a larger sonic

pattern. It is the pattern within the seeming randomness that you are after. Even a waterfall, which sounds at first to be wholly chaotic, betrays its patterns after one has honored it with a period of conscious listening. Once you detect a pattern, synchronize your purring, or your breathing, or both to it. This is the feline way of harmony.

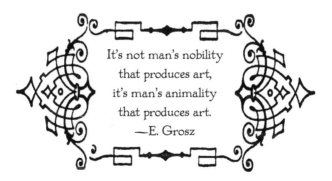

It's not man's nobility
that produces art,
it's man's animality
that produces art.
—E. Grosz

The Secret
of the Circle

To curl into a circle is to know centeredness. Indeed, as Euclid proved over two millennia ago, the shape of a cat's head mathematically points to the center of a circle. Take three points C, A, and T on a circle. The intersection O of the two perpendicular bisectors CA and AT is the center of the circle. The radius is OC.

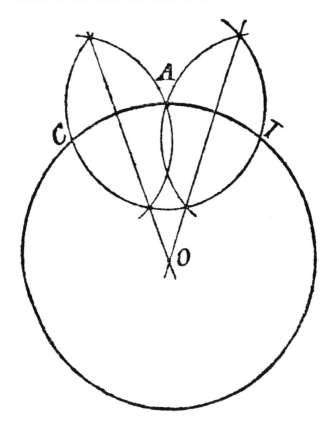

An Occasional Morsel of Catnip

To be perfectly healthy, a cat needs an occasional morsel of catnip. Sniff a sprig and you'll notice that it is the gray-green leaves and the flowering tops that are the most scented. The best time to collect this perennial herb is when the plant is in flower. Reject the tough stems and branches; dry the delicate flowers and the oval or heart-shaped leaves.

Often bitter to the taste, catnip tea is a mild stimulant, tonic, and emmenagogue. It also has a quieting effect on the nervous system.

The Power in
Just Sitting

By practicing sitting like the ancient sages, the mind is gradually trained, and unexpected events will finally not be able to astonish or trouble us. Nervous energy will not be uselessly wasted upon excitements or impulses. Equilibrium of mind will be maintained. This sitting technique is not meant to induce a trance state of self-hypnotism. It aims at keeping the mind well-poised and directing attention on any point one wills.

1. Sit down on a carpet or cushion. Or, lie on your back and stretch your legs as much as possible, then relax.

2. Open your eyes halfway, allowing them to remain unfocused. (This is known as the "lion's meditation.")

3. Count the number of breaths with your digits, to one hundred.

You are not bound to follow any particular method. You are free to choose a method for yourself. The general attitude is one of self-examination or introspection. It is not necessary to cogitate on the deep subjects of metaphysics, nor the virtues of a deity, nor the transitoriness of mundane life. It is merely an occasional withdrawing from the turbulence of worldliness and devoting some time to a quiet inspection of one's own consciousness. When this habit is thoroughly established, you can keep serenity of mind even in midst of a whirlwind. The aim is to allow your mind enough time for deliberation and save it from running feral. Indeed, this is the very impulse that separated the domesticated cats from their wild cousins. Just as we are drawn to watch from the higher places, so do we feel interest in higher things which are above the senses. The state of mind we pursue is neither full wakefulness nor

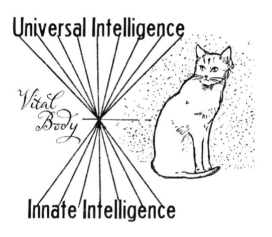

Universal Intelligence

Vital Body

Innate Intelligence

apathy but rather a calm concentration on breathing and the thought under consideration. One fosters cool-headedness, lucidity, and dispassionateness. The observing eye is steadied. Energy is kept in reserve; whenever demand is made, it will manifest itself with tremendous potency. Observed superficially, you may appear dull or dreamy, but you will be ready to work wonders when the occasion arises. It is only shallow waters, as the sages have said, that make a noisy, restless stream, while a deep whirlpool goes on silently. It is in the perfect mirror of consciousness that myriads of reflections come and go without ever disturbing its serenity.

Purring
and Healing

Vocalize an "ah" sound so as to make it hum or vibrate in the throat, prolonging the sound as long as you are able to do so in one exhalation. Purring is well-known for fostering self-healing, including the stitching of broken bones. That is because this vibration arouses every atom in the body, setting the entire system a jingle until the polarization of the body is entirely altered and reconstructed.

Turning Nature
Into an Open Book

Cats often quietly alternate open and closed eyes. This state of mind is known as restful alertness. It is neither sleepy nor alarmed, neither a state of drowsiness nor of focused attention. Restfulness and alertness coexist, as when one is eavesdropping. Repeating the process of opening the eyes for several moments, then closing them for several moments, you will begin to notice that when outer eyes are closed the inner eyes and the inner ears open. By opening the inner eyes and ears, nature becomes like an open book. Nothing can be hidden from the inner eyes and ears.

I gave up on thoughts altogether and let the animal within—the primeval essence of preservation— take over my body.
—C. T. Acadian

Hunter and
the Hunted

Greek mythology's huntress, Artemis, was transformed into a deer. That myth reveals an arcane truth, that hunter and the hunted are secretly identical. A cat carefully watches a field mouse, a snake, a lizard; what you place your attention on neurologically defines you. What we call separation is an illusion, and cats instinctively feel the oneness of all life. A cat can claim the field mouse, the snake, and the lizard because it knows their every next turn. A cat knows every next turn because it is not deceived by the illusion of separation.

Carefully study a mouse over the course of a day, then study a snake, and then a lizard. Continue your observations until you are convinced of the oneness of all life and begin to predict each animal's next move.

Waiting at the Mouse Hole: The Secret of Patience

Waiting patiently at a mouse hole offers a reward: the mouse. Time used to learn patience is never wasted. Therefore, take time to learn the art. Where and from whom can we learn? Everywhere and from a great many things around us. Learn from the trees, birds, flowers, insects, other animals, and all nature. The ant is a good teacher of this subject. The spider is an authority. No cat can learn patience except by going out into the bustling world and taking life just as it blows.

No Authority
But Oneself

In 1899, a sage wrote, "politics is like a snake in many things, but, particularly, in this: You can't hurt it by stepping on its tail. ... Strike for the head, the head of the party." Indeed, feline politics are anarchistic ("without ruler"). There are two platforms.

1. Freedom.

2. Autonomy (not being controlled by others).

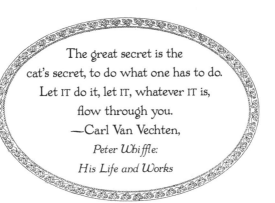

The great secret is the
cat's secret, to do what one has to do.
Let IT do it, let IT, whatever IT is,
flow through you.
—Carl Van Vechten,
Peter Whiffle:
His Life and Works

From out of these two platforms spring the following attitudes and behaviors:

a. The pursuit of self-interest.
b. Freedom to associate with those one chooses and to disassociate from anyone at will.
c. Acting for oneself instead of relying on others.
d. Cleaning up after oneself.

A cat's mind
a kingdom is.
—James Whitehead

The Difference
Between
a Cat and a Cat

The ancient Welsh Dimetian Code (also known as the *Book of Blaegwyrd*) specifies the difference between a cat and a cat. (Indeed, it is the same Welsh word in both instances.) The nine qualities of a cat are:

1. kills mice well
2. shall not devour its kittens
3. shall not go caterwauling on every new moon
4. without marks of fire
5. perfection of ear
6. perfection of eye
7. perfection of teeth
8. perfection of tail
9. perfection of claw

If these qualities are not met, then the animal is merely a cat.

Similarly, in the Venedotian Code, the qualities of a cat are "to see, to hear, to kill mice, to have her claws entire, to rear and not to devour her kittens."

Importantly, in the Gwentian Code, the tail, eyes, and life of a cat are considered of equal value.

"Cat's Cradle":
How to Play with Yarn

Cats instinctively know how to play with thongs of animal hide, yarn, twine, lines, cord, and rope. (Cord is a young rope, between string and rope in thickness. Twines and lines are forms of string. String is usually made from cotton, and rope is usually woven from yarn.) Playing with some type of string every day is vital to the process of becoming one's own cat. With a loop of string, you can form evocative figures such as "Cat's Eye" and "Fish in a Dish." (If you become a witch's familiar, you'll be glad to know that one German name for string games is *Hexenspiel*, "witch's game.") These games can be played by two, whom we'll call "A" and "B."

Hunt down a piece of string about the height of a man. Tie the ends together to form a single loop about three feet long. All string games begin with an opening, the object of which is to get the original loop so arranged on the hands that a number of secondary loops shall cross from the fingers of one hand to the fingers of the other. You'll begin with your hands held in what is called their usual position, namely, with the palms facing each other and the fingers directed upward. We'll use the terms "near," "far," "right," and "left" to describe the position of the strings as seen from the perspective of each player.

To form the initial "Cat's Cradle," "A" takes the string, passes the four fingers of each hand through the untwisted loop, then separates the hands until taut.

With the thumb and index finger of the right hand, "A" grasps the left near string and wraps it around the left palm and across the back of the left hand, bringing the string to the right between the left thumb and index. In the same manner, "A" wraps the right near string once around the right hand. There are now two strings across the back of each hand and one string across each palm.

At this point you can create what in Japan is called *Nekomata*—a domestic cat transforming itself into a mountain cat. In America, it is less-colorfully called "Fish Pond." Begin by picking up the segment across each palm with the opposing middle finger. There is now a loop on each middle finger and two strings across the back of each hand, the "Cradle" being formed by a straight near string, a straight far string, and the crossed strings of the middle finger loops.

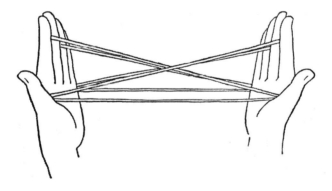

Now the left thumb of player "B" is placed under the "A's" near middle finger string, and the left index is placed under "A's" left near middle string. Then, by bringing the thumb and index together, "B" picks up between the fingertips the two near middle finger strings just where they cross at the near side of the figure. In the same manner, "B" picks up the two far middle finger

strings, by putting the right thumb under the right far
middle finger string, and the right index under the left
far middle finger string, then brings the thumb and index
together to hold the two strings where they cross at the
far side of the figure.

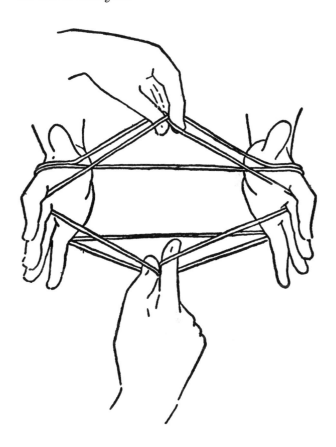

Now "B" separates the hands, drawing the
crossings away from one another, then down around the
untouched strings, and finally up into the center of the
figure.

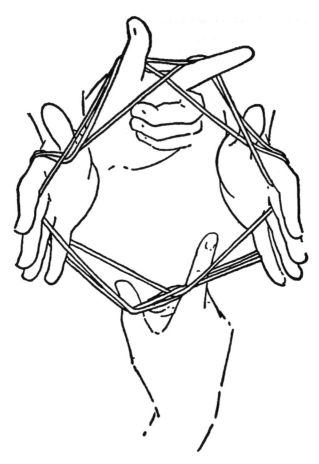

Then, by drawing the hands apart and separating the index fingers widely from the thumbs, "B" removes the figure from "A's" hands and extends the "Cat's Bed."

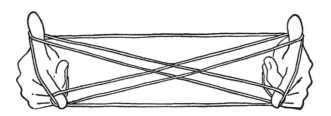

There is a loop on each thumb, a loop on each index, and a string passing across the backs of the thumb and index finger of each hand. The figure is formed of the four finger loops crossing in the middle, a straight near string and a straight far string.

From this you can form "Sphinx Legs." "A" inserts the left index finger from above into "B's" left thumb loop, near the center of the figure, and the left thumb from above into "B's" right thumb loop, and then, bringing the thumb and index finger together, picks up between the fingertips the far thumb strings just where they cross. In like manner, by inserting the right thumb from above into "B's" right index loop and the right index from above into "B's" left index loop, "A" picks up the two near index strings where they cross. "A" then separates the hands—drawing the right hand away from "B" over and past the near straight string, and the left hand toward "B" over and past the far straight string.

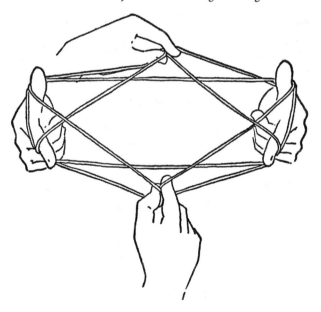

"A" finally puts the thumb and index finger of each hand (still holding the strings) under the corresponding side string and from below into and through the center of the figure, when, by drawing the hands apart and separating the index fingers widely from the thumbs, "A" takes the figure from "B's" hands.

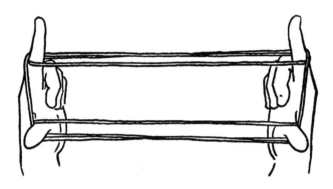

There is a loop on each thumb, a loop on each index, and a string passing across the backs of the thumb and index of each hand; the "Sphinx Legs" are formed by a straight single far thumb string, a straight single near index string, and straight double far index and near thumb strings.

From this you can form the "Upside Down Cat Bed." Standing to "A's" right, "B" turns the left hand with palm facing upward, takes up in the bend of the little finger "A's" near index string, and draws it over the strings toward "A." Then "B" turns the right hand with the palm up, taking up in the bend of the right little finger "A's" far thumb string and draws it over the other strings away from "A."

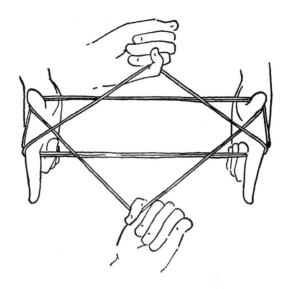

Closing the little fingers on the palms, "B" passes the left thumb and index from "A's" near side under the two thumb strings and up the center of the figure; at the same time, "B" passes the right thumb and index from "A's" far side under the two index strings and up the center of the figure.

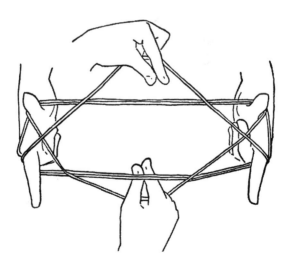

Then, drawing the hands apart, and separating the index fingers widely from the thumbs, "B" takes the figure from "A's" hands.

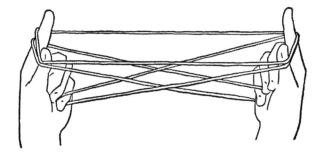

"B" now has two strings passing across the backs of the thumb and index of each hand and a loop held to the palm by each little finger. The form of the "Window Ledge" is the same as that of the "Cat's Cradle" only inverted.

From this, "A" takes the "Window Ledge" from "B's" hands in the same way as "B" took the "Cat's Cradle" from "A's" hands, but the thumb and index of each hand (holding between their tips the two crossed strings) are brought up around the corresponding side string and down into the center of the figure.

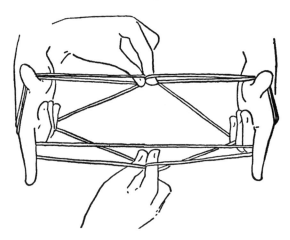

Then, when the hands are drawn apart and the thumbs and index fingers widely separated, "A" forms a figure exactly like the "Cat's Bed," but it is held with the fingers pointing downward.

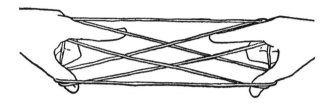

From this you can create the "Cat's Eye." "B" takes the figure from "A's" hands in the same way as "A" took the "Cat's Bed" from "B" to form the "Sphinx's Legs"; but although "B" has a loop on each thumb, a loop

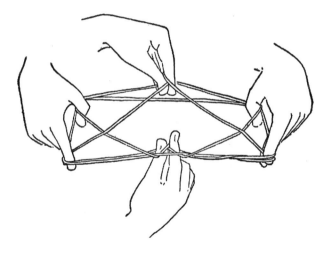

on each index, and a string passing across the backs of both thumb and index, instead of getting the same figure as the "Sphinx Legs," the "Cat's Eye" has two straight near thumb strings, two straight far index strings and crossed far thumb strings forming a central lozenge and four triangles produced by the thumb and index loops, which may be called the near and far right, and near and far left triangles.

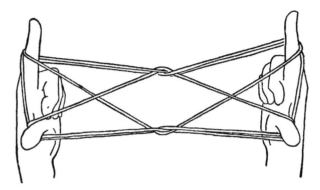

From this you can create the "Fish in a Dish." "A" inserts the right index from above into "B's" far left triangle, the right thumb from above into "B's" far right triangle, the left index from above into "B's" near left triangle, and the left thumb from above into "B's" near right triangle; then turning the thumbs and index fingers up into the central lozenge, "A" draws the hands apart,

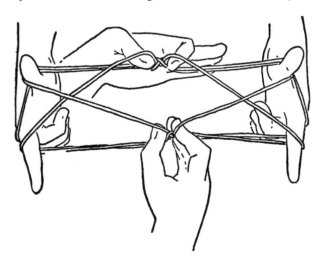

separates the index fingers widely from the thumbs, and takes the figure from "B's" hands.

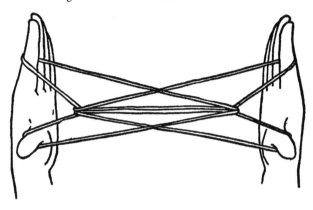

The "Fish in the Dish" consists of a large central lozenge, divided lengthwise by two straight strings and right and left near and far triangles. There is a loop on each thumb and a loop on each index, but no string passes across the backs of either thumbs or index.

From this you can form "The Clock" from the nursery rhyme, "Hickory dickory dock, the mouse ran up the clock." First, "B" arranges the two strings which pass from side to side through the central lozenge so that, uncrossed, they can easily be separated into a near string and a far string. Second, "B" now turns the left hand with the palm facing upward, picks up in the bend of the left little finger the near string which passes through the central lozenge, and draws it over the other strings toward "A"; then turning the right hand with the palm facing upward, "B" picks up in the bend of the right little finger the far string which passes through the central lozenge, then draws it over the other strings away from "A."

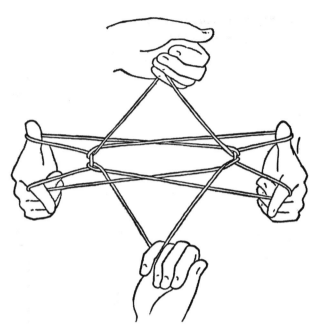

Putting the right thumb from above into "A's" right far triangle, the right index from above into "A's" left far triangle, the left thumb from above into "A's" right near triangle, and the left index from above into "A's" left near triangle, "B" turns the thumb and index of each hand toward the center of the figure and up into the central lozenge, when, by drawing the hands apart, and

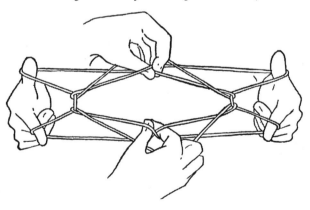

separating the thumbs widely from the index fingers, "B" takes the figure from "A's" hands. When the figure is held vertically, it represents the tall clock the mouse runs up.

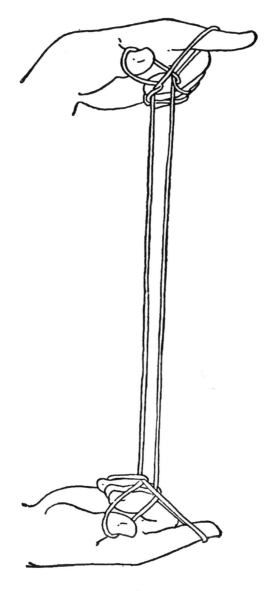

Improving
Night Vision

1. Avoid looking at any light source directly. Light sources diminish your night vision by forcing your pupils to contract. If a light source is unavoidable, cover one of your eyes. Your night vision will be maintained in that eye.

2. Allow your pupils to open fully by relaxing in perfect darkness for half an hour. Cover your eyes, if you wish.

3. Hone your peripheral vision so as to navigate through darkness using the rod cells of your eyes. Focus just off-center of where you are moving. Look through the corners of your eye to detect movements, shapes, and contrasts.

4. Travel low to the ground so that objects in your path will be backlit by the light of the moon, stars, and comets.

5. Enhance your night vision with your senses of smell, hearing, and touch.

6. Rest your eyes often. Allow them to remain closed for minutes at a time, massage them gently at intervals, and take short naps throughout the day.

7. In ancient Egypt, night blindness was treated with a
   prescription of diced liver.

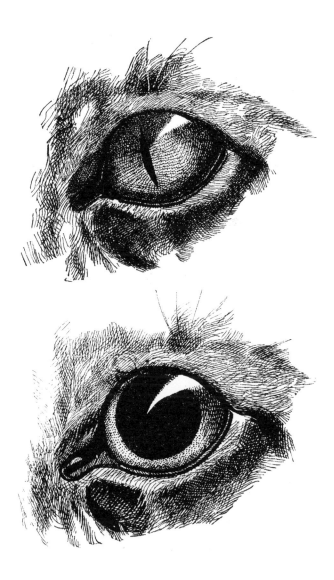

What Is and Is Not a Cat's Nature

Is:

> It is a cat's nature ... to accommodate itself to circumstances. —F. W. H.

Is not:

> It is not a cat's nature to be vengeful—or heroic. He merely does what is necessary to secure food, warmth, comfort, peace, and an occasional scratch behind the ears.
> —Lilian Jackson Braun

Is:

> It is a cat's nature to examine every inch of the house he lives in; and it is not possible to change a cat's nature. —Doris Bryant

Is not:

> It is not in the cat's nature to be a drudge.
> —John Rublowsky

Entitlement to Periods of Rest and "Me" Time

Here's a chart for planning your "Me" times of rest.

Reduce Your Age to Cat Years

Human Years	Cat Years
15-23	1
24-27	2
28-31	3
32-35	4
36-39	5
40-43	6
44-47	7
48-51	8
52-55	9
56-59	10
60-63	11
64-67	12
68-71	13
72-75	14
76-79	15
80-83	16
84-87	17
88-91	18
92-95	19
96-99	20
100-103	21
104-107	22
108-111	23
112-115	24
116	25

Discover for Yourself
the Truth of Cat Lore

Throughout history, cats have been credited with exalted souls and very special abilities:

- to see into the future

- to see into the human soul and to read people's thoughts (but to remain mute so as to allow others free will)

- to connect with the moon (which waxes and wanes like a cat's pupils)

- to see the spirit world (ghosts, fairies, and fantastical creatures such as unicorns)

- to look at the setting sun and optically retain its light

- to control tides, weather, and the growth of crops

- to hold the soul of an ancestor

- to impart clairvoyant powers

- to protect children from demons

- to shape-shift back into a witch

- to bring remarkable gifts

Through the process of becoming your own cat, you will be qualified to verify this lore for yourself.

Becoming a Cat
Down to the Molecule

You recall the quantum physicists finding that any two so-called discrete objects exchange electrons with each other. You recall the philosophers Deleuze & Guattari positing a sort of net of fibers that connect one to another, by which energies and informations are traded so as to invite "becomings." The soaring quality of music, they note, initiates a "becoming-bird" in a listener. Likewise, a person *can* transform into a cat, in very significant ways. It's not about imitation or merely identifying with a cat. "Starting from the forms one has, the subject one is, the organs one has, or the functions one fulfills, becoming is to extract particles between which one establishes the relations of movement and rest, speed and slowness that are *closest* to what one is becoming, and through which one becomes." It's not a question of "really" turning into a cat, nor of resembling a cat; nor is it a symbolic metaphor. It's about intensely establishing a proximity to a cat that makes it impossible to say where the boundary between human and feline lies. The state of "becoming-cat" is real, even though one does not necessarily grow a tail. You become-cat only if, by whatever means or elements, you emit particles that enter the relation of movement and rest of the cat particles. You become a cat only molecularly. You do not become a purring kitten, but by purring, if it is done with enough feeling, you emit a molecular kitten. It is from within you that a cat arches its back~not through imitation or analogy but the production of molecules. All becomings are molecular: a cat, too, is a molecular collectivity in a state of becoming~a cat becomes the mouse it stalks, the wall it hides behind, the sunlight it sleeps in.

Consider this related brain-twister: how is a racehorse less like a workhorse than a workhorse is like an ox?

Attribute	Workhorse	Ox	Racehorse
Pulls heavy burdens	x	x	
Dirty	x	x	
Tethered	x	x	
Moves slowly	x	x	
Work long days	x	x	
Crucial to farm production	x	x	
Well-groomed			x
Wins trophies			x

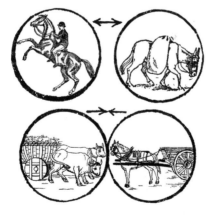

Likewise, a cat-person is more like a Persian cat than an indoor cat is like an alley cat. The science of ethology doesn't define a body by species or genus but rather counts affects. (This is an insight into how and why the owl and the pussycat are friends.)

Not to *Merely* Lie in the Sun

One of my greatest delights
was to ... lie in the sunshine
in the most absurd positions.
—H. B. Paull, *Only a Cat, Or, The
Autobiography of Tom Blackman*, 1877

And therein lies the most vital clue of all. It is the
positioning of absurdities that distinguishes a cat.

It is vain to deny that we are animal.
Make a lasting peace between your
spiritual self and your animal self.
There is no natural antagonism.
In truth they are in perfect harmony.
Your animal will submit kindly and most
helpfully to the control of your higher self,
if intelligently led and kindly treated.
—Kaxton

43715590R00038

Made in the USA
Middletown, DE
28 April 2019